A PATCHWORK OF PROMISES

30 Devotions for Quilters

by
GAYLE OTTEMILLER

SonRise Devotionals
Lighthouse Publishing of the Carolinas

A PATCHWORK OF PROMISES: 30 DEVOTIONS FOR QUILTERS
Published by SonRise Devotionals
An imprint of Lighthouse Publishing of the Carolinas
2333 Barton Oaks Dr., Raleigh, NC, 27614

ISBN 978-1-941103-83-8
Copyright © 2013 by Gayle Ottemiller
Cover design by Goran Tomic
Interior design by Karthick Srinivasan
Cover Photo: Cindy Sproles
Quiltmaker - Velma Frady, Kingsport, TN - First Frontier Quilt Guild

Available in print from your local bookstore, online, or from the publisher
at: www.lighthousepublishingofthecarolinas.com

For more information on this book and the author visit: www.gayleottemiller.com

Brought to you by the creative team at Lighthouse Publishing of the Carolinas:
Cindy Sproles, Marsha Hubler, Eddie Jones, and Shonda Savage.

Library of Congress Cataloging-in-Publication Data
Ottemiller, Gayle
A Patchwork of Promises: 30 Devotions for Quilters/ Gayle Ottemiller 1st ed.

Printed in the United States of America

Praise for *A PATCHWORK OF PROMISES*

If you're looking for a worship companion that's as warm and comforting as a line-dried quilt, look no further than *Patchwork of Promises*. Gayle Ottemiller delivers a sensitive, uplifting devotional that will wrap around you like the Almighty's tender love.

~**Loree Lough** – Bestselling author of 105
Award-winning books

Gayle Ottemiller stitches a delightful assortment of quilt stories together to create an artistic 30-day devotional to cheer, comfort, and challenge the hearts of quilters and those who wish they were. Each meditation ends with "Sew On," a pithy, time-saving quilting tip from author and speaker, Grace Fabian. It's a winner!

~**Patricia Souder** – Writer, Former Director of
Montrose Christian Writers Conference

A Patchwork of Promises will appeal to quilters. But the life applications from God's Word woven into the devotions will help and encourage women, old and young, whether or not they quilt.

~**Beth Westcott** – Writer, Pastor's Wife

I'm not a quilter; I can hardly even mend a sock! But you don't have to be skilled with needle and thread to be blessed by the wise words of this little book. As I read *A Patchwork of Promises*, I felt as though each devotional reading was another piece of a homemade comforter that I could wrap around myself and rest in. If you're seeking the warmth of God's promises, look no further.

~**Ann Tatlock** – Christy Award-winning author
Of *Once Beyond A Time*

A Patchwork of Promises combines heartwarming quilting anecdotes with soul-warming promises of God. Author Gayle Ottemiller's gentle spirit is stitched through each of the stories as intricately as the threads on a family quilt, inviting the reader to a quiet conversation that pieces earthly cares with God's love and provision.

~**Vie Herlocker** – Writer and Editor

TABLE OF CONTENTS

ACKNOWLEDGEMENTS

MANY THANKS TO Grace Fabian, former missionary, Bible translator, and quilter who so graciously contributed tips for *And Sew On*.

To the women's quilting group of Elmwood Presbyterian Church, Syracuse, New York. Thank you for your mission to the homeless and your passion for the art.

DAY 1

The Comforter Within
God Will Never Leave You or Forsake You

I will ask the Father and He will give you another comforter.
John 14:16 (The Living Bible)

THE FEATHER MATTRESS atop an already high bed required a step stool to reach the top. Before sinking blissfully into the mattress, I'd carefully choose a quilt from the foot of the bed and pull it up to my chin. The memory still brings comfort and peace.

Looking up from deep within that soft fortress, plastic glow-in-the-dark stars were scattered across the high-peaked attic ceiling. The sensation was one of pure happiness and peace.

In a cold and sterile hospital room, ten-year-old Emily shivers under the *Miss Kitty* quilt made by a stranger and dreams of home. The warmth of the simple covering slowly helps her feel secure.

In an urban nursing home, Jenny's ninety-seven-year-old fragile fingers tenderly stroke the lap robe laid across her knees. The stitching brings back memories of happier days when her hands fingered other fabrics creating similar projects for her family. Prayers the recipient might be comforted float to heaven.

The binding thread here is the comfort quilts bring to our lives at any age. From an aunt to her niece, or a stranger to a lonely child caught in chronic illness, to a group of women praying over their projects for the elderly; quilts bring added warmth and comfort to our lives. They express the love for others to the recipient.

God wants to convey His love for us. This love is so great He sent His only Son to die for us so we can have a relationship and everlasting life with Him. Before He left earth, Jesus said, "I will ask the Father and He will give you another Comforter." He has not left us alone to deal with life. It's one thing to be warm physically, but God wants us to have the personal joy, security, and strength of the Comforter within . . . the Holy Spirit.

Promise
He will never leave you or forsake you.

Sew On
Donate a quilt to your church. They make wonderful fundraisers in a silent auction.

DAY 2

Comfort Food
God Prepares a Table in the Presence of Our Enemies

You serve me a six-course dinner, right in front of my enemies.
Psalms 23:5 (The Message)

THE SCENT OF warm bread wafts slowly through the room like thread drawn through a needle. The fresh-baked loaf would be a tasty addition to the simple lunch Mom made for a picnic at the park.

It was a rainy day, and our disappointment showed. Not quite the fun, sunny day in the park we'd anticipated for the past week. To make up for our loss, Mom spread a favorite quilt over the living room floor and carefully placed the fresh bread from the oven accompanied by jars of peanut butter and jelly, apples, chocolate chip cookies, and glasses of cold milk for our impromptu indoor picnic.

We settled in to enjoy the simple meal. We all sat cross-legged on the floor with our favorite comfort foods served in a safe, dry environment. Mom saved the day again.

That simple meal spread out on a favorite quilt brings sweet memories, but God prepares for us an even better table. Psalms 23:5 (The Message) says *He serves a six-course dinner, right in front of my enemies.* What could be better than that? Scripture reminds us Jesus is the Bread of Life. He is the perfect comfort food for the hungry soul. Fresh bread that celebrates good times, sustains us in lean times, and helps us through hard times.

It gets even better. When we receive Jesus into our hearts by faith, God has promised and has prepared to serve us a divine banquet in heaven—a triumphant meal celebrating life and overcoming death. His provision is better than anything we could ever experience here on earth.

Promise
He serves up a banquet in the presence of our enemies.

Sew On
When you have finished your quilt top, spread it across the bed or floor. Then use a lint roller to go over it to pick up any pesky threads or lint. Now you're ready to quilt it.

DAY 3

Controlled Chaos
God is in Control

*A handful of peaceful repose, better than two fistfuls
of worried work.*
Ecclesiastes 4:6 (The Message)

A WELL-KNOWN TELEVISION teacher casually tosses leftover scraps of fabric over her shoulder and into a corner as she works. I always wondered what happens to those pieces. As insignificant as they seem, they are tiny bits of quilting history.

Never toss those scraps away. If they aren't used in another quilt they could become part of a scrapbook page, a potholder, a beautiful handmade card, a doll's quilt, or even laminated and made into a brooch or pin. Some quilters bag the scraps and trade with others to gain more variety, or they donate the scraps to missionaries who then give the scraps to be made into beautiful projects to sell. The proceeds from the sales, in turn, feed the hungry.

Think of the fragmented pieces of our lives. Sometimes we feel like we've been shredded into a thousand pieces and tossed into a corner like discarded fabric pieces.

As a child born with physical disabilities, I felt forgotten and rejected by my peers. Unable to join in many normal activities, I frantically sought a place to fit in. Maybe God had forgotten me too. Maybe He couldn't ever use me. But He could use me…and He did.

Never fear. God knows exactly where each piece is and how

to use it to create something beautiful out of chaos.

Think about the billions of stars in the sky or intricate snowflakes, even grains of sand . . . no two alike, sparkling like tiny diamonds on the shore. God created everything in the universe, not to mention you and me. Our thousands of project pieces are not hard for Him.

Scripture says to *cast our cares* onto Him for He cares for us. Imagine that . . . the God of the universe emptied Himself of divinity and came to earth to be one of us. He knows what it's like to be human. He knows the worries and weaknesses of the world. He takes all of that and more as we give it to Him. Yet through it all, He still makes something beautiful of our lives and makes us useful for His kingdom.

Promise
God is in control . . . always.

Sew On
Save all those bits of fabric left from your quilt. Use them
for making another quilt with smaller blocks for a
wall hanging or placemats.

DAY 4
Dream on Joseph
God has a Dream for You

Listen for God's voice in everything you do, everywhere you go.
Proverbs 3:6 (The Message)

STRIPES HAVE LONG been popular. Pinstripes, wide stripes, wavy stripes. Stripes running vertically on a garment make the person appear taller and thinner. Stripes placed horizontally? Not so slimming. Twelve-inch blocks of stripes set alternately in a quilt would thrill a child.

Stripes are everywhere in nature. Think about the rainbow—points of refracted light thrown across the sky. I think God was having fun one day and said, "Put this color next to that one, then this one over here." He rolled the rainbow out like a bolt of fabric and said, "Done." It looked so good He put stripes everywhere . . . on zebras, tigers, raccoon tails, watermelons, glaciers . . . even on skunks.

Man looked at all those natural stripes and said, "Wow, let's weave some stripes." So Joseph ended up with a striped coat of many colors. He must have felt pretty special . . . like royalty.

Dream on, Joseph. He held on to that dream from poverty to prison. When Joseph told his older brothers about his dream, they ridiculed him and finally sold him into slavery. From pit to pinnacle Joseph held on to his dream. God gave it to him. Maybe he couldn't see how things could ever work out through his circumstances, but he knew God well enough to trust Him with his life. God could make a way, and He did.

God still gives dreams today. He gives hope where it seems hopeless, makes a way in the desert, and parts the sea of our circumstances. He gave a dream to Joseph and to so many others throughout the ages, and He can do it today.

Promise
God dreams big for you.

Sew On
When making identical blocks, perhaps you need 16 log cabin blocks. Sew the first seam on all 16. Chain-piece them together to save thread and time, then press the seams of all 16 at the same time.

DAY 5

Ebony and Ivory
God Doesn't Leave Anything Unfinished

*In this world you will have trouble. But take heart! I have
overcome the world.*
John 16:33 (New International Version)

KEYBOARDS STRIKE JUST the right note in ebony and ivory.
Pandas and penguins are perfectly suited in black and white.
Okay, how about skunks? Life would be easier if all the choices
we have to make were that clear.

A black and white quilt that was supposed to be finished
months ago still waits patiently as "fat quarters" in . . . you guessed
it! A black and white fabric covered box.

All of the sewing implements are ready for service, but the
project takes low priority. Life rudely interrupted my plans.
Carefully chosen fabrics and complementary stitches will bring
the design to life someday, and this project will be complete.
Hopefully.

Contrast and choice make up the fabric of our lives. Light
and shadow enhance each other. It has been said that on the
darkest night, stars shine brightest.

Life doesn't always work out the way we want or plan. We
diligently set our goals and schedule. Then when the goal, like the
quilt, is laid aside for one reason or another, we complain. Bitterness
fills us. We may even give up entirely. We don't live in a trouble-free
world, nor does God promise a life full of joy and gladness. On the

contrary, Jesus told us we would have trouble while here on earth, but He is always with us. He will never leave us.

As we trust God every day, He is faithful to guide and direct us. We have His word He will never leave us nor forsake us. We can be sure that in all things, God is in control. He has a plan and purpose and might just take our plans far beyond anything we could ever dream or imagine, right out of this world.

Promise
God doesn't leave anything unfinished.

Sew On
When choosing print fabrics for two-color quilts, include small, medium, and large prints for variety and interest.

DAY 6

Fan the Flame
He has Given a Gift – Exercise it

I remind you to fan into flame the gift of God which is in you.
II Timothy 1:6 (New International Version)

SEVERAL OLD, FOLDING fans of varying materials and sizes have come down through our family. Silk, paper, even carved ivory, gloriously display the cooling mechanisms of earlier days. Women used these handmade fans for various occasions, some for everyday use while others were used on fancier occasions. One beautiful white, silk fan was part of my paternal grandmother's wedding outfit. Another intricately carved ivory fan is a mere 2 1/2" and hangs from a delicate ivory necklace.

Other fans made from wedges of cotton print fabrics compose a quietly designed quilt pattern laid out on an ivory-colored field.

Designed to provide a cool breeze, fans soothed the user on a hot summer day. Women fanned the embers of a fire into the flame with them as well.

Paul wrote: God has put into you a precious gift. In fact, He's given you more than one. He has given you life. He has given you the opportunity to choose eternal life through His Son, Jesus, and He has given you talents and specific creative abilities with which you can bless others.

Have you ever thought of the gift you have in your hands? Not just the final gift you create in the form of a quilt but the gift of encouragement or of service to others. Don't let those gifts go to waste. Make time to fan the flame.

When you teach others the art of quilt-making you are "fanning the flame," and God is pleased.

Promise
God gives to each one a talent.

Sew On
Tack a sandwich bag to the end of your ironing board. Inevitably, you'll find stray threads, fluff, thread tails or fabric scraps as you iron. This prevents tripping over one more waste can.

DAY 7
The *Father-Heart* of God
This is the Nature and Nurture of Abba Father

Look at the birds...careless in the care of God. And you count far more to him than birds.
Matthew 6:26 (The Message)

THE DELICATE, TRANSPARENT wings of dragonflies flitting or the shapes of flying geese charting a course across a queen-sized quilt remind me of a favorite nature preserve where bevies of bugs and birds share an environment perfect for exercise and inspiration.

Before Dad passed away, our family enjoyed many excursions through that world, admiring and respecting all of God's creation.

On a recent spring visit to the preserve, ducks and ducklings, dragonflies, and redwing blackbirds greeted me once again. A fine Canadian gander and his mate drew protective parentheses around yellow goslings. Water lilies littered the surface of the marsh, forming a resting place for birds and hiding place for fish.

A great blue heron stood regally at waters' edge, preening its wings. A neatly coifed dark-feathered head topped its white-capped neck and shoulders. Slowly, he unfolded a long slender neck. A dagger-like beak designed for spearing completed the striking silhouette.

Spotting a fishy entrée, the heron turned towards the marsh. On the back of his head was a perfect heart shape—exactly what I needed that day.

God shows us His heart just when we need it most. He knows

us intimately, and He cares deeply for us. He knows when we hurt or just need encouragement. The heron reminded me of that.

Canadian geese migrate thousands of miles each year with a programmed flight plan. Great blue herons intuitively know the best dining spots. Look at the birds of the air, careless in the care of God. We can be sure our Father is well aware of our circumstances. He holds us firmly in the palm of His hand and always in His heart. We can trust Him with everything that concerns us.

Promise
God loves you . . . this is the nature and nurture of Abba Father.

Sew On
Take photos of every quilt you complete. Carry the album with you to validate bragging rights.

DAY 8

Father Knows Best
He is the Author and Finisher of Our Faith

Listen for God's voice . . . he's the one who will keep you on track.
Proverbs 3:6 (The Message)

LIFE AND QUILTING are easier when we follow the directions. "But I'm directionally challenged," you say. "I'd rather go my own way and do it myself. I don't need directions."

"Ah, this looks easy. I'll just go ahead and do it my way." Famous last words. Maybe that's how crazy quilts got started, and the craze just carried on. When will we ever learn?

Men do this all the time. Why follow the map when you can just follow your intuition or your nose? You don't have to be a rocket scientist to know when you have written directions, it's better to take a look, make a plan, and follow step-by-step what someone has taken the time to provide you. It's much easier in the long run.

Why don't we want to follow directions? Perhaps it's pride. And what is the central letter in that word? "I".

God has given us powerful directions for life in His guidebook, the Bible. Why don't we take the time to read it? Perhaps you've said: "I don't have the time. I'd rather go my own way. The Bible isn't relevant for today." But God's Word is relevant for today . . . for us.

God made you. Psalms 139 reads: *You know me inside and out...You formed me in my mother's womb.* Jeremiah 29 reads:

I know the plans I have for you. Furthermore, our opening Scripture reminds us to listen for God's voice, and He will keep us on track.

How many times have we asked what to do in a situation? Well, ask. God is more than willing to respond.

Promise
He is the author and finisher of our faith.

Sew On
If you've made a mistake, use a seam ripper to undo the seam.
Then use tweezers to clean away all the
tiny threads before re-stitching.

DAY 9

Fits or Fruit
He is the Vine, We are the Branches

The fruit of the Spirit is love, joy, peace, patience, kindness,
goodness, faithfulness, gentleness and self-control.
Galatians 5:23 (New International Version)

IT WAS ONE of those days. Actually, one in a string of bad days. Love, joy, peace, patience, and kindness were not high on Sue's priority list. Deciding to relax with a bit of sewing, she picked up the pile of fat-quarters for her latest project and discovered some were missing, or rather, borrowed. She discovered her daughter had used them for a school project. So much for relaxation time. Sometimes she felt like she was having more fits and less fruit.

She needed something to change her dismal mood. Perhaps a new project—a placemat project with bright colors.

When you're wrestling with a "down" time, how about taking time to work on a project with bright citrus colors such as lemon, lime, and orange? If you add other fruit colors like cherry, strawberry, grapefruit, they cheer you up, don't they? Try making a table runner or placemats or maybe an apron. Try something that will pull you out of the pits and make you fit for fruit cocktail.

God wants His children to bear a special kind of fruit, the fruit of the Spirit: love, joy, peace, patience, kindness, goodness, faithfulness, gentleness, and self-control. Our rich, ripe fruit should sweeten relationships, build up others (and ourselves), and bring spiritual growth to a family. Last, but not least, our fruit should gladden the heart of God. This is the fruit of the Spirit. Just as it takes time for natural fruit to grow on the vine, you'll find it's a slow process but worth the work. Don't try to do everything at once. Be patient. God certainly is patient, and He isn't done with you yet.

Remember, at the heart of the fruit is the seed. Put God first and plant His word in your heart, mind, and soul every day. Fresh fruit is bound to come.

Promise
Jesus is the Vine. We are the branches.

Sew On
Organize your fabric by color and by type: geometric, solid, batiks, etc.

DAY 10

Fresh Bread
Jesus is the Bread of Life

The bread of God is he who comes down from heaven.
John 6:33 (The Message)

THE AROMA OF baking bread pressed into my senses like a seam beneath a hot iron—warm and unforgettable. Crisp, cotton cloth lined a basket holding more fresh-baked bread. Irresistible!

What could be better than a gathering of friends meeting together to bake bread, to talk up a storm, and maybe to exchange patterns or fabrics? You supply the ingredients for bread baking, and your friends can bring add-ins and a good family recipe (or box mix). Afterwards, in a semblance of a modern-day quilting bee, everyone can exchange quilting tips and materials as well as share recipes and friendship.

Sometimes all it takes to bring a community together is to break bread together or sew a quilt to be donated to a family who has lost their breadwinner.

The apostle John identifies the bread of God as "...*he who comes down from heaven,*" Jesus Christ. Luke 11:3 instructs us to pray for God to give us this day our daily bread. A hearty, nutritious, full loaf of fresh-baked bread lies waiting in the written word of God.

Feast on the Bread, which is full of life. Choose a thick, rich, mouth-watering, hunger-slaking slice. Don't go for the crumbs under the table. God sends an open invitation to taste and see that He is good.

Bread of Heaven*
Taste and see that he is good
He offers you celestial food.
He fills your hunger quenches thirst.
Accept his love...his blood.

From *Faith Lifts: When Life Lets You Down*
©2010 Gayle Ottemiller

Promise
Jesus is the Bread of Life.

Sew On
Start an "Ask Your Neighbor" column in your local paper,
inviting others to join a "fabric exchange." You'll save money
and make some great friends.

DAY 11
Fussy-Cutting
God Knows Full Well When to Cut and Delete

You know me inside and out, you know every bone in my body.
You know exactly how I was made, bit by bit, how I was sculpted
from nothing into something.
Psalms 139:15 (The Message)

"I DON'T UNDERSTAND. What exactly is 'fussy' cutting? Aren't we just being a little too picky?"

"That's not exactly it," the teacher patiently explained. "Fussy cutting is following the detailed edge of a pattern design such as a floral motif or animal. The cutting heightens the outline of the design, and the shape will stand out when appliqued onto a background fabric."

Fussy cutting can be very tedious work. To master the technique, consider making a pillow cover at first instead of a queen-size quilt. How about a tote bag or eyeglass case?

Starting a project like this may cause us to consider God's "fussiness." For thousands of years, He has been *fussy cutting* the details of the universe, so many details that scientists still haven't got it all figured out, even when they like to think they have.

Then when we consider our own circumstances, what do we do? We complain over a little fussy cutting. The Bible calls this process "pruning." Sure, there are problems, but God isn't finished fussy cutting yet. His Word tells us He'll complete that good work He started. When He's finished, Jesus is coming back.

That's a promise. He'll continue the pruning process until He has all of the details surrounding our lives finished and highlighted.

Thus, in the light of eternity, who am I to fuss about snipping a few details into some fabric pieces or God clipping some sense into me to live more faithfully for Him?

Promise
God knew you before you were born. You are fearfully and wonderfully made.

Sew On
Before going ahead with the full quilt, make one sample block. Do the colors blend? Do the patterned pieces combine nicely? Is there a contrast of colors to give it richness? Too busy? Is it the right size? Do you even like it? Your practice piece can easily be made into a potholder or cushion cover if you're unhappy with it as a first block.

DAY 12
The Golden Thread
He Binds Everything Together Perfectly

We can be sure that every detail in our lives of love for God is worked into something good.
Romans 8:27-28 (The Message)

It was love at first sight. Grandma's crazy quilt was a kaleidoscope of color, texture, pattern, and shape. Velvet nestled near silk, cotton calms satin. Scraps of children's clothing, lace from a wedding gown, and the wide end of Grandpa's tie were all added. The crocheted corners of handkerchiefs lay comfortably together.

I watched Grandma's fingers patiently pinch three strands of gold thread through the eye of a needle. Intricate stitch patterns outlined each patch, joining them together. The quilt was painstakingly crafted with love and prayer. The finished masterpiece pleased the eye, mind, and heart—bound as one by the beautiful golden thread.

That's how God patterns our lives. Individual days and events sometimes seem random. They just don't seem to fit. Some experiences we would just as soon toss away while others, we'll never forget. Yet, God is near, and we find encouragement in Romans 8:28. God promises . . . *every detail in our lives of love for God is worked into something good.*

God created all things. He imagined the initial design for all our lives and sees it through from the first stitch to the last. The pattern, fabric, and texture were all chosen before we were born – and God has vested interest in the final product.

What is the final product? God gave His Son who lived and died as one of us so we can become all the Father wants us to be. Finally, the Holy Spirit came to complete God's work in us.

As we lay our lives before God, He patiently pieces together a pattern pleasing to His eye. With Jesus as our foundation, our lives demonstrate the plan the Master envisioned from the beginning of time. The completed work will reveal the golden thread of His inspiration.

Promise
God works everything together for the
good for those who love Him.

Sew On
Easily pull three strands of embroidery thread together through the eye of a needle by folding a strip of paper over the thread ends, slide the paper sandwich through the eye.

DAY 13
Hiding Place
God is a Safe Haven

God is a safe place to hide, ready to help when we need him.
Psalms 46:1 (The Message)

MY VERY ENERGETIC kitten takes a break every now and then to sleep off a round of chase-your-tail by sliding under the black and white queen size quilt. She thinks no one can see her even though the moving lump in the middle of the bed does look suspicious. Undercover cat at work.

Practically every child has used a sheet or quilt as a tent hung over a clothesline or pinned around the backs of chairs. And what child hasn't retreated to his room under a handy quilt with a favorite stuffed animal to enter a world of dreams?

Quilts make wonderful cocoons. A comforter is a wonderful haven when needed. It's still my favorite place to retreat in times of stress. In fact, all of us yearn to have a place of comfort … a place of solace, especially during times of stress.

God knows our deepest needs and has provided that comfort, one who can always be trusted in time of need. Jesus reminded us if we ask the Father, He will give us another Comforter. This Comforter, the Holy Spirit, dwells within every believer who has received Christ as Savior. We have a Comforter and a safe haven to hide in when the world is too much for us. This is God's promise to those who trust Him.

Have you done that? He is ready and willing to enter that

relationship with you.

Promise
God is a safe haven.

Sew On
If there is no selvage, keep a little square of the fabric and a record of where you bought it. In case you run out of fabric, having a record will help you find more of what you need. Search at www.findmyfabric.com if you still can't find it.

DAY 14

How Does Your Garden Grow?
Good Soil Produces Good Fruit

The seed cast on good earth is the person who hears.
Matthew 13:23 (The Message)

GRANDMOTHER'S FLOWER GARDEN was the most popular quilt pattern. A 1925 sewing book, *The Romance of the Patchwork Quilt*, reads, "If quilts have taken the country by storm, then the hexagon Flower Garden, or Grandmother's Flower Garden… is a whirlwind." The pieces lend themselves to endless color combinations and ways the blocks could be set together. There could potentially be thousands of pieces in a quilt. It takes lots of time and patience to produce such a masterpiece.

One single wreath of 12 hexagons made its way into my collection of unfinished projects. I can't imagine what it would take to piece together thousands of these tiny shapes.

A beautiful quilt requires time and sometimes the patience of Job to be properly constructed. Just as a natural garden must be cared for and nurtured to reach its potential, so does the detailed work of a quilt.

Seeds must be sown in good soil. The garden needs plenty of sunlight and water, and weeds removed. Full, mature growth for the plants requires a watchful eye, time, and effort.

The process is the same for the Christian walk. When God's Word is planted in good soil, the hearer must be ready to listen and respond. God usually speaks to us through scripture and prayer. But to hear God, we must be attentive for His voice.

Essentials to growth are receiving the Light of the World (Jesus) and living water (the Holy Spirit). Weeds (sins) are removed by an active relationship with Jesus. It takes time and effort to grow and mature as a Christian.

Promise
Good soil produces good fruit.

Sew On
Grandmother's Flower Garden makes a wonderful, quick and easy project such as a potholder, decorative design, or tote bag. A hexagon-shaped template made of cardboard is an easy pattern to duplicate.

DAY 15

Mission Possible
The Field is White Unto Harvest

Give to your neighbors in trouble,
your poor and hurting neighbors.
Deuteronomy 15:11 (The Message)

MAYBE IT'S NOT possible for you personally to go into all the world, but there are plenty of opportunities to enter the mission fields all around you. As soon as you open your front door, the mission fields await.

The Lutheran World Relief Quilt Campaign is one such mission outreach. This organization describes its outreach to "not only comfort someone you have never met, but provide an object that is useful in ways you probably never imagined." Quilts are used as baby carriers, as market displays spread on the ground and piled with vegetables, or simply as a constant reminder that someone far away really cares.

Quilters, please consider getting involved in this or another project. There's no need to leave home to be a missionary. Think about it. Wouldn't you be a grateful recipient of the caring work of others halfway around the world or across the street?

Christ said to go into the entire world and spread the gospel. A quilt or other quilting project can carry the love of Christ to places you might never see in person. Christ's mission was to seek and save the lost. He gave His followers the same commission. Allow the Holy Spirit to work through you by caring for your neighbor as well as those who live around the globe. The Bible challenges us to serve and in turn, we are served in times of need. The satisfaction you'll receive in serving others with your talents will be payback enough. That's a promise.

Promise
The field is ripe unto harvest.

Sew On
Missionaries around the world have taught quilting to women who need financial help. Consider donating fabric from your stash to help these entrepreneurs.

DAY 16

Morning Star
Jesus is the Light of the World, the Bright Morning Star

Wait for daybreak and the rising of the
Morning Star in your heart.
2 Peter 1:19 (The Message)

THE SUN BEGAN to rise on Mt. Sinai. The deeper purples on the granite surface of the mountain faded to an intense lavender. We had already climbed for more than three hours.

Billions of stars in the blackened sky faded as the morning star took its place on the edge of the universe. Stone colors melded into blue, red, yellow, and finally white as the sun rose higher on the mountain. A song of praise rose from those who had made the journey and climbed the hard places. It was more than worth the struggle, far beyond anything many of us had ever dreamed we would accomplish.

What dream has God given you? To make an award-winning quilt or finish one your mother started many years ago? Perhaps you need to complete a project around the multiple needs of a growing family or design and carry out the task of creating a 50th anniversary quilt for a special couple. Maybe your dream is to participate in a project to send 50,000 quilts to the poor around the world.

Think about it. God, the Creator of the universe, has put in you a core of creativity. He has a plan and purpose for your life. There is a myriad of ways to use your talents and have the challenge and fun of creating a practical work of art.

Peter tells us God's word is *a light shining in a dark place, until the day dawns and the morning star rises in your hearts.* Wouldn't you want to reflect that light … to be a shining light for Jesus? You can do that in the beautiful things you create. You may have to climb a few mountains to get there, but the view from the top is spectacular.

Promise
Jesus is the Light of the World.

Sew On
Choose your fabrics in natural daylight. Color is distorted under florescent light bulbs.

DAY 17

Patterned After God
When We See Him We Will be Like Him

So shall we bear the likeness of the man from heaven (Jesus).
1 Corinthians 15:49 (New International Version)

EVERY AWARD-WINNING QUILT starts with a great design and a carefully executed pattern. The finished product depends on carefully following directions. You wouldn't take a quick look at the pattern pieces and toss them aside. A beginning quilter wouldn't tackle a complicated pattern. The experienced quilter considers every aspect of the task and determines the final cost of the project in time, money, and skill level.

Consider Amish quilters, the plain folk, who use hand stitching throughout the whole project. A single quilt can take hundreds of hours to complete, taking a practiced eye and hand, focus, clear thinking, patience, and long-suffering for the long view. It doesn't happen in a day.

The book of Genesis tells us we are made in the image of God. We are not little gods, but we are patterned after Him . . . made in His image. That doesn't mean we look like Him; rather, we will have His characteristics. As we walk in faith, we grow to be like Him. 1 Corinthians reads, "So shall we bear the likeness of the man from heaven (Jesus)."

God uses Jesus as our pattern for living. Therefore, look to Jesus and keep your eyes fixed on Him. As you study God's word, obey what it tells you. Change those things that don't reflect

His image and character. Let your mind be renewed, and your actions mirror those of Christ.

Promise
When we see Him, we will be like Him.

Sew On
Lay out your finished blocks. Look at them frequently for the next couple of days. Keep rearranging them to be more pleasing. Squint at them. When your eyes draw to the one that sticks out, remove it.

DAY 18

Piece by Piece
He Who Began a Good Work is Faithful to Complete It

Each day has enough trouble of its own.
Matthew 6:36 (The Message)

SHARON PLANNED TO spend most of the day pulling together the final stages of her current quilting project, a special gift for her mother- and father-in-law for their 50th wedding anniversary. She had spent months contacting friends and family, collecting special messages to incorporate into the design. Each message would be in the donor's own handwriting and hand-stitched onto ten-inch squares. One beautiful, final project held generations of love.

The day started as planned but quickly deteriorated. One thing after another took time and mental energy, and before long, half the day was gone with no end to her project in sight.

"Life isn't long enough to get done all that I have to do. I'll never finish this project," Sharon exclaimed. "Enough is enough."

Tell me you haven't felt like that too. You look at the enormity of the task ahead, and it's overwhelming. This was supposed to be fun, relaxing, enjoyable, but it takes forever to finish. *What was I thinking?* One more project is pushed aside for another day.

Did God feel that way when He started to create? He had the entire universe for a final project and just seven days to complete it. Was it too big a job for Him? Absolutely not. "Little" human projects, our hurts … desires … prayers are not too hard for Him to handle. He knows we are finite. We have issues and problems that can overwhelm us, even if it's just a simple quilt project. God knows we easily get derailed by life. However, if we proceed one day at a time with His strength and help, nothing is too difficult. As we continue, God reminds us not to get worked up about tomorrow. God will help you deal with whatever difficulties that might come, and He will guide you when the time comes.

Promise
He who began a good work in you is faithful to complete it.

Sew On
Put your name and date some place on each quilt.
You've earned it.

DAY 19
Pillows and Pillowcases
He Will Make You Lie Down in Green Pastures

You will have the poor with you every day for
the rest of your lives.
Mark 14:7 (The Message)

THERE'S A DIFFERENCE between pillows and pillowcases. You lay your head on a pillow while a pillowcase protects that headrest of comfort filled with "whatever." The *whatever* could be cotton batting . . . or a stone. How do you see the two? What is your perspective?

Most Americans have no difficulty providing pillows and pillowcases. They have enough resources to supply them for their families. But in other parts of the world, many people have no place to lay their heads, not to mention a pillow to support their head. Those in many Third World countries would give anything to own a pillow. For them, dirt is the mattress, and a stone is their pillow. Jesus had no place to lay His head.

Think about it. The Son of God, who would soon give His life for those who ignored, ridiculed, and abused Him, left everything in heaven to redeem a fallen and sinful world . . . to redeem you and me. He saved us, gave us a spiritual pillow on which to rest our heads, and left instructions to help the poor any time we desire.

Are you willing to help? Do you care enough to give a pillow or pillowcase to someone sleeping in the streets?

Promise
He will make you lie down in green pastures.

Sew On
If you don't have time to make a full quilt or coverlet to give, quilted pillows or pillowcases are good alternatives for the homeless.

DAY 20

Plain and Simple
Tranquility and Peace are the Rhythms of Grace

Are you tired? Worn out? Learn the unforced rhythms of grace.
Matthew 11:28-29 (The Message)

SERENITY, PEACE, QUIET living. Plain and simple—this is the lifestyle the Amish people have cultivated since the beginning. Their handmade quilts, often taking hundreds of hours to complete, embody the philosophy of those who create them.

The words of an old Shaker hymn come to mind: *Tis a gift to be simple* ... quilts by Amish women utilize techniques and technology used 150 years ago. Needles and thread are employed by the women to painstakingly produce bed coverings and wall hangings. Using traditional solid colors or neutrals and geometric shapes on a black background, the quilts reflect the simplicity and grace of the Amish home and lifestyle.

Amish quilts reflect the love and care of the women who make them. Created to be gifts to mark weddings or births, quilts are produced by one woman (or several), during sessions called "bees."

In today's culture, packing as many activities as possible into the day seems to be the norm. Technology replaces handcraftsmanship. Multi-tasking replaces attention to detail. Nothing is simple anymore. Tranquilizers and treadmills replace tranquility. But our Lord Jesus says, "Slow down!" Cultivate the quiet harmonies of life, not the hectic pressures.

Learn to appreciate the quiet simplicity of a sunrise, the

beauty of a rose, the sound of rippling water. Touch a kitten's fur and listen to it purr. Jesus tells us in Matthew 11: *Walk with me and work with me, watch how I do it. Learn the unforced rhythms of grace.* (The Message).

Start your day reading God's word and wait long enough to listen to His heart. Ask Him to quiet your pace and remind you throughout the day what your priorities should be. Treat others the way you want to be treated. Speak words of encouragement to those around you. Offer assistance when needed.

Promise
Tranquility and peace are the rhythms of grace.

Sew On
Enjoy the process. Don't be in such a hurry that you miss the pleasure of creating.

DAY 21
Prayer Quilts
God Hears and Answers Prayer

Before they call out I will answer.
Before they finish...I'll have heard.
Isaiah 65:24 (The Message)

MANY CHURCHES HAVE quilting ministries. Some combine these practical ministries with a prayer ministry as well. Prayer is powerful.

If you are in a quilting ministry, keep your focus on the recipient of the quilt. Remember why you are making it. One resource available for ideas is *www.prayerquilting.org*

Prayer quilts may be small or large, simple or complex. More important than how the quilt is made, is the prayer lifted up on behalf of the recipient. Some quilters prefer to tie their quilts rather than sew the layers together. A prayer for the recipient covers each lovingly tied knot. The recipient can rest assured that untold numbers of prayers are covering them.

Our scriptural mandates to bring everything to God in prayer are serious. How serious are we to live a life of faith that pleases the Lord and endures until the end?

God makes His intention and passion clear in the book of Isaiah: "Before they call out I will answer. Before they finish speaking, I'll have heard." If He would do that for a nation, how much more will He hear and answer those for whom His Son died?

Promise
Lord, I know You hear and answer prayer.

Sew On
It is important to sew a label in a quilt . . .
identifying it as a prayer quilt.
This allows everyone to see it and know its purpose.

DAY 22
Purple, Scarlet, Gold, and Blue
Royalty Came to Earth as a Common Man

Give them fine linen cloth, gold thread, and blue, purple,
and scarlet thread.
Exodus 28:5 (New Living Translation)

ROYAL COLORS, COLORS fit for a king . . . bold colors that make a statement. They are rich, confident, strong colors that say, "I'm taking my stand and I will not move." Well, maybe a quilt would say, "I'm not taking this lying down" and would rather make a great wall hanging.

After mentioning the brilliant colors for a quilt, we could also say the same about clothing fashioned into a classic jacket. Velvets and silks might be embroidered in gold and silver like my grandmother's Victorian crazy quilt. Why not?

How about a banner for your front door, a tote bag, a vest, or a cover for your PC, tablet, or smartphone?

The world invests so much time and energy in drab electronics, forcing us to live with the gadgets or be left behind. Why not spice up your life with bold, rich color . . . maybe in small quantities at first. Make a special, unique masterpiece to express who you are in this modern age.

When God mentioned fine linen cloth and deep, richly colored and metallic thread in His Holy Word, He referred to Aaron and his three sons called to be priests. They wore sacred garments of many colors fit to wear while ministering to the Lord in the Tabernacle.

In the New Testament, we are called a royal priesthood. Shouldn't we be able to wear richly embroidered garments too?

Promise
Royalty came to earth as a common man and lives forever as a King.

Sew On
If you need a softer shade or more subtle tone for a block, try using the backside of fabric.

DAY 23

Quilting for Others
Comfort One Another as You Have Been Comforted

Pray to your Father in private, then your Father, who sees everything will reward you.
Matthew 6:6 (New Living Translation)

ENCOURAGEMENT IS A much-needed commodity today. We spend a great deal of time on social media and cell phones, often paying more attention to the electronic face in our hands and ignoring the flesh-and-blood face in front of us. But those of us who dare step away from the "norm" still use our hands to create a unique and artistic presentation of color and texture.

The act of quilting affords the opportunity to slow down, think about, and pray for the potential recipient. Maybe you don't have anyone specific in mind or any special event or opportunity, but prayer will give you direction. He may have the perfect person in mind to receive the special gift. While you're sewing, without losing track of what you're doing, meditate on the word of God hidden in your heart. Even God loves quilts. He is creating them every season on the earth He created. Have you looked at our land from an airplane? Have you seen pictures taken by satellites farther out in deep space? The globe on which we live is exquisite with complex components that contribute to the grand design.

Promise
Encourage and be encouraged.

Sew On

Keep a list of possible people or organizations for placing
your quilts: children's hospitals, newborn wards,
nursing homes, Veterans' homes or homeless shelters,
day-care centers, or new neighbors.

DAY 24

Quilt of Remembrance
Remember What the Lord Has Done for You

He remembers His Covenant…He's been as good as his word.
Psalm 105:8 (The Message)

IT WOULD BE a great project . . . the celebration of my parents' fifty years of marriage. The anniversary would not be for ten months, plenty of time to plan and develop a particularly special memento . . . a quilt of remembrance.

I'd contact all our relatives and friends. Each would receive a square of muslin with instructions to design, draw, or, at least, describe something of significance for the anniversary couple. Each square would contain the printed or script signature of the giver. Younger grandchildren would be encouraged to create their work of art on drawing paper first and transfer it later. All the squares would then return to me for final assembly and construction of the quilt—kept as a secret from my parents until the final celebration.

All went well until a few weeks before the anniversary celebration when things went painfully wrong. Mom died of a sudden heart attack. I regretted that I hadn't started sooner and let her in on the surprise so she could have enjoyed the planning and process.

The point is not to wait to make a quilt. Many special events deserve a quilt of remembrance such as anniversaries, birthdays, graduations, and sports accomplishments.

Psalm 108 tells us that God remembers His covenant for a thousand generations, referring to His covenant with the nation of Israel. But He's been as good as His word concerning His care for us as well. We are reminded He who began a good work in you will be faithful to complete them all. I'd like to think He has a memory quilt of our lives too.

Promise
All of God's promises are yes and amen.

Sew On
You can heat-transfer photographs onto your quilt by following the directions on the transfer paper package.

DAY 25
Quilts of Valor
The Joy of the Lord is Our Strength

Every time I think of You, I give thanks to my God.
Philippians 1:3 (New Living Translation)

COMING HOME! WONDERFUL words for our servicemen and women and their families.

As quilters, commit to pray and give thanks for our military personnel and their service to our country, providing encouragement and God's protection for our troops. The Quilts of Valor Foundation is an organization dedicated to collecting, creating, and distributing handmade quilts to service members and veterans. The quilts made by groups internationally welcome home veterans and comfort those hospitalized from severe injuries and deep emotional scars.

The Quilts of Valor volunteers seek to soften the inevitable side effects of war. The finished projects are both a tangible and warm thanks for our military personnel coming home from war or for those who have served in other wars. 1 Thessalonians 5 tells us to *pray all the time – thank God no matter what happens. This is the way God wants His believers to live...*

Sew on! Realize that you are making a difference in the life of someone who is possibly giving his life for you . . . and remember the One who willingly gave His life for each one of us on a cross over 2000 years ago.

Promise

This is how much God loved the world; He gave his Son, His one and only Son. And this is why: so that no one need be destroyed; by believing in Him, anyone can have a whole and lasting life.

John 3:16 (The Message)

Sew On

Press seams to one side. It makes for a stronger seam than if you open the seams.

DAY 26
A Short Shirt Tale
God Has a Memory Quilt of Your Life

He will remind you of everything I have said to you.
John 14:26 (New International Version)

JUST TRY TO throw out that T-shirt with a favorite logo, the one from that awesome concert, or the one with your adolescent's super-hero. Impossible? I thought so until I realized the shirts had some redeeming value.

Why not make something of them? How about a quilt that Mom patches and presents to her child the first day of college?

Most every child has a collection of T-shirts representing important events. Consider giving your child a warm quilt to cover him when he's far away from home. It's better than letting those old T-shirts collect in a pile on the closet floor or land in the trash bin.

Cut the shirtfronts in squares and alternate them with coordinating solid colors or cut closely around the images with embroidery scissors and applique them onto a solid color foundation. You could frame one very special shirt with a mat of coordinating colors for a distinctive picture to hang on the dorm-room wall.

God reminds us daily that He loves us by His creation that surrounds us. The sun rises in the morning and the moon shines by night. Scripture tells us the trees will clap their hands and rocks cry out if we fail to tell of God's love. Your children need to know that God, and you, love them. Perhaps a personalized T-shirt quilt will confirm that in your children's minds.

We all need reminders of good times and good experiences sometimes just to make it through the day. Encouragement is good for the soul and spirit.

Promise
God has a memory quilt of your life.

Sew On
Secondhand clothing stores like Goodwill, Salvation Army, and The Rescue Mission have good shirts for sale. Cut off frayed collars cuffs and seams. Press and cut out squares for your next high style, low-priced quilt.

DAY 27

Ties that Bind
A Strong Cord Cannot be Easily Broken

A three-stranded rope isn't easily snapped.
Ecclesiastes 4:12 (The Message)

THERE ARE TIMES we become so bound and determined to get something done that we can't get started. What project or goal has you all tied up in knots? Don't be *fit to be tied*. Loosen up. A project doesn't have to be heavily embroidered or intricately quilted to be beautiful. Use DMC or crochet thread rather than yarn that fuzzes up and can pull out.

One of my favorite birthday presents is a lap quilt my niece made by using soft pastel colors. The top, batting, and backing are tied with three strands of white embroidery thread. Simple but effective. The technique also works well for a T-shirt quilt, giving a more casual look to complement the style.

Tying the layers together at regular intervals prevents the layers from slipping. Using a single strand is not enough. Two or more strands are best to keep holding things together. It's important that knots are secure so they cannot be pulled out during normal use and washing.

Scripture describes a three-stranded rope with respect to relationships. The full verse cited above tells us, "By yourself you're unprotected. With a friend, you can face the worst. Can you round up a third?" Having natural, flesh-and-blood friends is wonderful. But the best friend anyone can ever have is Jesus.

An old hymn reminds us of that wonderful relationship with our Lord and Savior: "What a friend we have in Jesus…"

Have you asked Jesus into your heart? He will hold you together in the normal "washing," the daily wear and tear, and in the storms of life.

Promise
A strong cord cannot be easily broken.

Sew On
Depending on the batting/filler/middle, be sure there are enough knots to hold it together and to keep the middle layer from shifting around. If one is using flannel or warm and natural batting, one knot every ten inches is adequate. If using a fiber that is "loose," a knot every four inches works best.

DAY 28

"Ugly" Quilts
The Lord Looks at the Heart

Humans look at outward appearances,
the Lord looks at the heart.
1 Samuel 16:7 (New International Version)

SINCE ITS BEGINNING in 1985, the Boston Ministry Project* has volunteers making homemade sleeping bags called the "Ugly Quilts" for the homeless of New England. A warm sleeping bag is a great alternative to quilts on a cold night. This is a beautiful example of a ministry to men, women, and children who do not have a place to call home.

Every now and then someone starts a project, and before long, she wonders what she was thinking. It just doesn't look right. It's not that the quilt is ugly per se, but the color choices or the position of prints in the design do not measure up to the quilter's expectations. In this case, beauty *is* in the eye of the beholder. The quilter has a choice—rip the project apart or enter it in an Ugly Quilt contest.

You may be disappointed in your piece, but have you ever seen a truly ugly quilt? Humans tend to judge everything ... including one another. Many view the homeless people as inferior. Maybe they got where they are because of addictions or illicit behavior. Perhaps they deserve what they have.

Our way of assessing others or situations is displeasing to the Lord. Scripture teaches us our looks aren't everything, and we shouldn't be impressed. God and His judgments are different from ours. Humans look at the face, but God looks at the heart.

Take a moment and look at things the way God does. There but for the grace of God go I.

Promise
God's promise to us is simple: to love us with an everlasting love.

Sew On
Do you need a felted quilt wall to hold fabric in place as you audition squares and design your quilt? Instead of buying an expensive one, tack up a felt-backed tablecloth.

www.tbmp.org

DAY 29

Unfinished Business
God Isn't Finished With Us Yet

There has never been the slightest doubt in my mind that God who started this great work in you would keep at it and bring it to a flourishing finish on the very day Christ Jesus appears.
Philippians 1:6 (The Message)

MEMORIES AND TEARS flooded as I sifted through my mother's belongings. I had to laugh when I came upon a sizable stack of quilt blocks, patterns, and fabrics dating from the 1940s.

I get my procrastination honestly . . . from Mother. How ironic that Mom's incomplete projects now lay solely in my hands.

Sunbonnet Sue and the Boy with Fishing Pole hand-stitched to a muslin backing awaited. I saw the boy casting his fishing line across my brother's bed while Sue waited, wearing her neat bonnet and crisp cotton dress on my bed nearby.

Why didn't Mom finish the quilts? It didn't take long to figure out. Bill, her first-born, was followed by Johnny, who died in infancy. I came along with serious birth defects, and later, Bill was confined to bed for three years with rheumatic fever. Mom had her hands full.

She needed time to grieve, to heal, and to sit quietly. She needed to fill her mind and hands with something other than sick kids. So she began the quilts, but there was no time to finish.

In true family tradition, I can't count the times I've started with the best-laid plans and lofty intentions of crafting a beautiful award-winning quilt in record time. Yet it never happens.

Do you suppose God feels that way too? With four words, "Let there be light," He created a stunning world, intricately designed and detailed with perfect timing, perfect balance, and temperature and light controlled.

Then He created us. To top it off, He gave us free will. But God hasn't left any of us in a stack of unfinished projects. He's not done with us yet. He grieves when His creations are damaged or appear flawed, but God still maintains full control over the finished plan.

Promise
God isn't finished with us yet.

Sew On
You aren't artistic? If you need a picture, find your patterns in a children's coloring book. The patterns can be reduced in size or enlarged on a photocopier.

DAY 30
Warm Hearts, Willing Hands
We Are His Hands and Feet on Earth

He brings us alongside someone else
who is going through hard times.
2 Corinthians 1:4 (The Message)

PEOPLE NEED ONE another. Quilting provides a multitude of ways those who are passionate about their craft can connect with those of equal interests.

Perhaps it's even more valuable to find someone in the quilting community who is going through tough times and who may just need a break. Getting together to work on a project gives the participants a common goal, a way to connect quilt pieces as well as each other. It's relaxing, tension releasing, and fun.

Maybe you could make lap quilts for a local nursing home, crib quilts for newborns, or a project for a shelter for abused women.

Whether you're sewing to release your own tension or that of others, the end result is to create something of beauty and practicality.

Working in the community for a common cause enriches us. It gladdens the heart of God. Perhaps it was His idea to begin with. *Affection for others, exuberance about life, serenity . . . we develop a willingness to stick with things, a sense of compassion in the heart...and a conviction that a basic holiness permeates things and people.* (Galatians 5:24-25 The Message)

We are placed on this earth for a reason. Each of us is essentially in the same boat. Why not help one another and create something to make the world more beautiful in the process?

Promise
We are the body of Christ on earth. We are His hands and feet.

Sew On
The quilting pattern should complement the quilt top, adding to the overall impact.

Piece By Piece

You are God's workmanship made in His image. Every stitch of your life was designed and set in place before time began by the Master Craftsman. Each color, texture, and print reveals the imprint of His hand.

You are still a work in progress, a quilt of remembrance. We are looking at the underside of the project. Just keep in mind that God isn't finished with you yet. He will tie it all together in His time.

The quilt of your life is one of the most precious legacies you can leave to your family . . . to the world. Let it be one that brings honor and glory to the King of all Kings.

Happy Quilting,
Gayle

Gayle C. Ottemiller has published magazine articles, poetry, and devotions. Her work appears on ChristianDevotions.us and in several compilation books. Her book of poetry and photography, *Faith Lifts: When Life Lets You Down,* was published in 2010. Gayle has an MS in guidance and counseling and is retired after working for twenty-eight years with developmentally disabled adults. Find her on Facebook and LinkedIn.

Made in the USA
San Bernardino, CA
25 November 2018